Notes on English Literature

General Editor: JOHN HARVEY

Lecturer in English, University of Keele,
Staffordshire

Chaucer's Prologue
to the Canterbury Tales

RALPH W. V. ELLIOTT

Senior Lecturer in English Literature
in the University of Adelaide

BASIL BLACKWELL
OXFORD

First Printed 1960
Reprinted 1963

PRINTED IN GREAT BRITAIN
BY A. T. BROOME AND SON, 18 ST. CLEMENT'S, OXFORD
AND BOUND BY THE KEMP HALL BINDERY, OXFORD

GENERAL NOTE

This series of introductions to the great classics of English literature is designed primarily for the school, college, and university student, although it is hoped that they will be found helpful by a much larger audience. Three aims have been kept in mind:

(A) To give the reader the relevant information necessary for his fuller understanding of the work.

(B) To indicate the main areas of critical interest, to suggest suitable critical approaches, and to point out possible critical difficulties.

(C) To do this in as simple and lucid a manner as possible, avoiding technical jargon and giving a full explanation of any critical terms employed.

Each introduction contains questions on the text and suggestions for further reading. It should be emphasized that in no sense is any introduction to be considered as a substitute for the reader's own study, understanding, and appreciation of the work.

CONTENTS

viii   *Contents*

IV. Chaucer's Art 42
   1.   Language and Metre   42
   2.   Chaucer's Style   47
   3.   Chaucer's Art of Portraiture   56
   4.   Chaucer's Humour 63

V. Conclusion   68

VI. Further Questions   71

VII. Further Suggested Reading 72

I. THE WRITING OF THE PROLOGUE

1. *The Occasion*

The Prologue to *The Canterbury Tales* describes a company of English men and women come together by chance one April day in the fourteenth century in a London inn for the common purpose of making a pilgrimage to the shrine of St. Thomas à Becket in Canterbury cathedral. This was nothing unusual at that time, and the author of this particular description, Geoffrey Chaucer, may well have taken part in just such a pilgrimage and met the very people whom he describes. We know of some definite instances of pilgrimages which followed the same route, and the Pilgrims' Way through Dartford, Rochester, and Sittingbourne must often have been thronged by men and women (and sometimes children) of all types and classes riding or walking to Canterbury. But even when Chaucer was not himself engaged on such a pilgrimage—and some people, like his Wife of Bath, went quite often—he had plenty of opportunity to observe persons of the kind he describes. He spent a good deal of his time on official business in Kent, which meant riding through villages and small towns where lived craftsmen and merchants and ploughmen such as we meet in the poem. And in London, where Chaucer had lived for many years, every social group and every trade and profession had its representatives.

But is it necessary to assume that every or even any person described in Chaucer's Prologue represents a definite contemporary of his? It is the poet's privilege to let his imagination roam freely, so that quite often one character may combine a number of personal features observed by Chaucer in several different people, or even invented altogether. Some scholars have worked very hard examining documents of Chaucer's time in order to identify some of the pilgrims among his contemporaries and some of the results are really exciting. But as our main concern is with the Prologue as a poem the question whether Chaucer used actual people for his portraits doesn't much matter at this stage.

There is more point in asking why he wrote the Prologue at all; or, what was his intention in creating this fourteenth-century portrait gallery? The idea, as the word ' Prologue ' implies, was to introduce in some way the stories which follow it and which make up the bulk of *The Canterbury Tales*. To bundle a lot of stories together in one work was nothing new then, and to-day we are just as familiar with books of fairy tales or short stories. Nor was Chaucer the first to think of linking his stories in some manner by introducing us to the tellers and making these somehow interesting too. Most of us know the story of Queen Scheherazade who saved her life by telling, night after night for a thousand and one nights, the stories of *The Arabian Nights* and whose fortune becomes just as interesting to the reader as the stories themselves. Chaucer probably knew the *Decameron*, a collection of a hundred tales by Giovanni Boccaccio, written between 1348 and 1353, which bears some general resemblance to *The Canterbury Tales* and which he may well have come across during one of his two or three official journeys to Italy. Another Italian work, in which a number of tales are told to a company of men and women of various ranks and occupations journey-

ing about Italy to avoid the pestilence of 1374—the
Novelle of Giovanni Sercambi—may also have been
known to Chaucer and suggested some further hints
for the framework of *The Canterbury Tales*. But there
are such important differences between these works and
Chaucer's, above all the detailed, life-like, dramatic
portraits which make up the bulk of the Prologue, that
they cannot properly be considered as sources of
Chaucer's masterpiece. Many of the stories of *The
Canterbury Tales* admittedly make use of familiar
medieval story-material which Boccaccio and Sercambi also used, although Chaucer's accomplished re-
telling made them once again fresh and interesting, but
the Prologue remains his own brilliant and original
invention, unique of its kind in English literature.

The last point we want to note here is Chaucer's
choice of a pilgrimage to bring the story-tellers
together. It was a brilliant choice because on such a
pilgrimage people of many classes met in a holiday
mood, especially in spring with the hardships and
deprivations of a medieval winter behind them, ready
enough to entertain each other in the manner suggested
by Chaucer's Host, with stories that were to range
from animal fables to knightly adventures, and from
jolly tavern scenes to the pathetic martyrdom of a
young Christian saint.

2. *The Scheme*

It is in the Prologue that the scheme of *The Canterbury Tales* is outlined for us by the Host of the Tabard
Inn where the pilgrims assemble. Each pilgrim was to
tell two tales on the way to Canterbury and two on the
return trip to London, the prize for the best set of

stories being a free supper for the winner, the Host
acting as judge (788–809).[1]. Chaucer didn't get very
far with this scheme; perhaps it was too ambitious
to carry out fully, for it meant at least 116 tales,
perhaps he was too busy with his official duties, or
perhaps he even lost interest after a time. In any case,
he did not live to complete *The Canterbury Tales*. Only
twenty-three pilgrims get a turn, one each except for
the poet-pilgrim himself who has two shots and even
some of the tales we have are unfinished.

However, it is clear that from the very beginning
part of Chaucer's idea of *The Canterbury Tales* was to
introduce a number of different tellers for the different
tales. This number was twenty-nine:

> Wel nyne and twenty in a compaignye,
> Of sondry folk.   (24–5)

Unfortunately some confusion has arisen over the
number of pilgrims because in lines 163–4 we are told
that the Prioress was accompanied by another nun,
her *chapeleyne* (perhaps the religious equivalent of a
private secretary or lady-in-waiting), and *preestes
thre*. This would make thirty-one pilgrims, clearly a
mistake, so that we must assume either a slip of the pen
on Chaucer's part, or a line left unfinished and later
completed in this unarithmetical way by some careless
copyist. Perhaps Chaucer, having just completed his
portrait of the Prioress, was not anxious to describe
another nun straight away, so he just put her in her
right place intending to fill in her portrait later on,
and then forgot all about it.

[1] All the line references to the Prologue and quotations from it are taken
from the second edition of The Works of Geoffrey Chaucer by F. N. Robin-
son, published by the Oxford University Press in 1957.

Among the twenty-nine pilgrims Chaucer includes himself, which is a brilliant touch because it turns the whole pilgrimage at one stroke into a very credible eyewitness account, made all the more credible by Chaucer's apologising to us for any shortcomings of which he may be guilty in his reporting (725–46), and by countless little devices, such as telling us who rode with whom or what time of day it was, as well as by describing the pilgrims to us in detail. We shall see later on just how much of the delight and humour of the Prologue derives from the poet's putting himself among the pilgrims.

The Host is not included among the twenty-nine pilgrims. He is not introduced until near the end of the Prologue when he suggests his scheme of story-telling for the journey and proposes to join the company himself, making thirty people in all to set off from the Tabard Inn.

Chaucer's idea of *The Canterbury Tales* was therefore both more complicated and much more interesting than a simple collection of unconnected short stories: Against the background of a pilgrimage to Canterbury he introduces a number of potential story-tellers, himself among them, whom he endows with life and vitality and numerous individual characteristics, so that the whole work becomes interesting and dramatic. The Prologue is the first scene of this drama. In it we are introduced to the actors who are going to entertain us later on, not only with the stories they tell, but also with their own sayings and doings in the passages that link the tales.

The order in which Chaucer introduces the pilgrims in the Prologue is not arbitrary; it is part of the scheme, as also is the fact that later when it comes to the story-telling this order is turned all topsy-turvy by the fact that some of the rougher pilgrims barge in out of turn. Quite properly, in view of his chief rank among the secular pilgrims, the Knight and his attendants (Squire and Yeoman) come first. This little group is followed and balanced by one of the same number among the clerical pilgrims, namely the Prioress and her attendant Nun and Nun's Priest, for the Prioress ranks highest among the church members present. As an immediate contrast to the worthy nuns there follow the portraits of the very worldly Monk and Friar.

Then we switch back to the lay pilgrims, to the Merchant who represents a powerful and wealthy class of fourteenth-century society. Contrasted with him is the poor, studious Clerk of Oxford who is again one of the churchmen.

The Sergeant of the Law and the Franklin follow; they travel together.

The next group is that of the Five Gildsmen and their Cook who belong together, followed in turn by three other lay pilgrims who are much more sharply individualised: the Shipman, the Doctor, and the Wife of Bath.

Chaucer now returns to the churchmen with the portrait of the good Parson, whose Christlike holiness contrasts sharply with the boisterous worldliness of the Wife of Bath. The Ploughman follows, for he and the Parson are brothers.

The Miller and the Reeve are birds of a feather, despite their very different looks, but Chaucer separates their portraits by that of the Manciple, perhaps to stress the distance which these two quarrelling ruffians keep throughout the journey.

Two unredeemed ecclesiastical pilgrims, the Summoner and the Pardoner, conclude the portraits, except for the poet himself, and the Host who is not strictly speaking one of the pilgrims, although as one of the chief actors he is rightly introduced to us in the transitional passage between the portraits themselves and the start of the pilgrimage and the story-telling.

The effect of Chaucer's arrangement is to suggest (1) variety of character, appearance, and profession among the pilgrims; (2) contrasts or balance between one group of pilgrims and another; and (3) further lifelikeness to the whole situation by connecting certain pilgrims because they are friends, or relatives, or one is in attendance upon another.

For further reading: Part III, chapter 3, ' Pilgrims and Pilgrimages ', in *English Wayfaring Life in the Middle Ages*, by J. J. Jusserand, translated by L. T. Smith, 3rd edition, London, 1925; and chapter 2, ' Realism and Artifice ', in *Chaucer and The Canterbury Tales*, by W. W. Lawrence, Oxford University Press, 1950. For details of the parallels between the Prologue and the scheme of *The Canterbury Tales* and the works of Boccaccio and Sercambi see chapter 1, ' The Literary Framework of the Canterbury Tales ', by R. A. Pratt and K. Young in *Sources and Analogues of Chaucer's Canterbury Tales*, edited by W. F. Bryan and G. Dempster, University of Chicago Press, 1941.

3. *The Date*

As Chaucer kept no diary we don't know for certain when he wrote the Prologue. Nor does the exact year matter for us provided we can form an approximate idea.

Until 1386 Chaucer held several what we would now call civil service appointments in London and lived in a house over Aldgate. When in October 1386 this house was leased to someone else Chaucer had probably already moved to Kent where he was a justice of the peace and had just been made a ' knight of the shire ', that is a member of Parliament, just like the Franklin of the Prologue (355–6). In 1387 Chaucer appears to have travelled to Calais on official business, but we don't know how long he was abroad.

It is generally accepted nowadays that Chaucer began working on *The Canterbury Tales* during this period between 1386 and 1388, while he was free from regular office duties in London and spent a good deal of time riding about Kent on both private and public business. In 1389 he received another responsible and busy post, as Clerk of the King's Works, but as he retained his residence in Kent he probably revisited the county at intervals, perhaps making use of these visits to carry on with the composition of *The Canterbury Tales*.

If then we conclude that the Prologue was written between 1386 and 1388 we shall not be far out, and we have one further useful piece of evidence within the poem to confirm these dates. Speaking of his Merchant Chaucer says in 276–7:

> He wolde the see were kept for any thyng
> Bitwixe Middelburgh and Orewelle.

This can only be a reference to the fact that between 1384 and 1388 the wool-trade between England and the continent was conducted through the port of Middelburg on the island of Walcheren on the Dutch coast instead of, as usually, through Calais. As Controller of the Customs Chaucer would know such a detail and it is characteristic of him to reproduce it accurately. This fact thus adds weight to the composition of the Prologue falling between 1386 and 1388.

For further reading: The three biographical chapters (1, 4, 8) in *The Poet Chaucer* by N. Coghill, Home University Library, Oxford University Press, 1955; or chapter 2, ' The Life of Chaucer ', in *A Chaucer Handbook* by R. D. French, 2nd ed., New York and London, 1947. A very readable book which treats Chaucer's life and work as a whole is *Geoffrey Chaucer of England* by Marchette Chute, London, 1951.

Questions:
1. What can a knowledge of Chaucer's life contribute to our understanding and appreciation of the Prologue?
2. What reasons can you give for the order in which Chaucer introduces the Canterbury pilgrims to us in the Prologue? What would have been the correct order of fourteenth-century social precedence?

B

II. Religion in the Later Fourteenth Century

1. *The Religious Background*

As the Prologue introduces us to a company of people about to set forth on a pilgrimage to a much venerated English shrine, we will take a brief look at the religious background of an age in which such an event was an important and not uncommon occurrence.

In the last quarter of the fourteenth century the Roman Catholic Church continued to claim the undivided allegiance of all Christian people in Western Europe. In everything that people thought and did the importance of their faith and of the Church which fostered it was evident. The Church was visibly represented in all parts of the country by buildings ranging from splendid cathedrals, like that at Canterbury, to humble parish churches in small villages, as well as by religious houses, some of them rich and superbly laid out abbeys, others hardly more than hermitages. And everywhere you went you met men and women of the Church, preaching, or engaged on monastic business or on a pilgrimage, or just out for their own pleasure or profit. It is no accident that of Chaucer's twenty-nine pilgrims nine were professional members of the Church.

But the Church was not only outwardly in evidence. In their hearts people believed, often in a simple, childlike manner, what they were taught by priests and preachers about God and the world, about heaven and hell, paradise and damnation, angels and devils. The more earnest tried to live their lives according to the often very demanding precepts of Christianity, some in the dedicated lives of monasteries and convents, others in their trades and professions. But the ideals of the

Christian religion have never been easy to live up to, so that then as now men and women often fell far short of them, and the results were indifference, superstitions, and abuses of the kind which Chaucer so vividly describes in some of his pilgrims.

Indifference meant that some people did not care about the consequences of their actions, despite the Church's insistence that sins called for punishment and that unrepentant sinners would be damned to suffer the torments of hell. It meant that some people would cease to be serious in their chosen vocations, especially religious vocations in the priesthood or among the monastic orders. And it would mean that religious observances like prayers or pilgrimages or attending church services would no longer be felt to be very important and indeed were sometimes neglected or, like pilgrimages, regarded as holidays.

Superstitions are often quite close to genuine religious convictions, perhaps even more so during the Middle Ages when most people believed quite sincerely in miracles or dragons or in the influence of the stars on men's fortunes. One way in which this simple credulity manifests itself is in the manner in which abstractions like Envy or Patience or Death were often endowed with bodies and given human attributes in medieval paintings and books and morality plays as well as in the thinking of ordinary people. Normally superstitions don't do much harm, but in Chaucer's time, as the Prologue shows, there must have been a good many unscrupulous persons who exploited the simple faith of credulous people and their leanings towards superstitions. Chaucer's Pardoner, who claimed that the pillow-case which he carried about with him in his bag was Christ's mother's veil and that some of its miraculous powers could be bought for cash (694–5), was playing on the superstitious credulity of his customers with all the persuasive skill of a modern confidence trickster.

That there were many abuses in the life and work of the Church in the later fourteenth century is also evident from the Prologue. They took many forms, but underlying them all was a desire for personal gain, whether in the shape of wealth, or personal honour, or greater material comfort. Chaucer's Monk enjoyed hunting a great deal more than the studious seclusion of his cloister (177–85), and the Prioress is as aware of worldly esteem (139–41) as the very worldly Wife of Bath (449–52) or the equally aspiring tradesmen's wives mentioned in lines 376–8. And as for the desire for gain, does it not speak out of some of the clothes worn by pilgrims pledged to simple and austere living, or the unscrupulous dealings of others, whether men of the Church like the Friar and Pardoner, or engaged in secular callings like the Shipman or the Miller? There were quite a few among Chaucer's twenty-nine pilgrims who were ready to ignore both the teaching and the warnings of their Church for the sake of personal profit, and we can be sure that Chaucer was not exaggerating.

On the other hand, there were those who took their faith and observances more seriously, like the Knight who hastens to Canterbury to give thanks after his latest campaign, or the Parson whom Chaucer singles out as a model of righteous and unselfish living. Chaucer is always ready to give praise when he finds occasion to do so.

It so happens that the result in both cases is the same, for whether Chaucer is criticising or commending people's conduct he is drawing attention to their relationship with the Church and stressing the latter's importance in his time. It is because the Church was still so much the centre of medieval society that Chaucer includes nine ecclesiastical pilgrims among his company and devotes more than three hundred lines of the Prologue's 858 to the description of the seven of them of whom we have portraits. As professional churchmen and women they would attract attention not only as individuals, but as representatives of the Church, and as we shall see Chaucer packs a good deal of criticism into these seven portraits. Although he makes allowances where he can for individual human foibles and weaknesses, he speaks out boldly against corrupt institutions like the selling of pardons, for which the Church itself was primarily to blame. The contrast with the lay pilgrims is obvious, for they are not representatives in the same way: the Miller may not be scrupulously honest, but there is nothing wrong with milling as a trade, and similarly with the other crafts and professions. This is not to say, of course, that the church pilgrims are somehow *types* and the others not; far from it, but Chaucer does seem to suggest that while an irresponsible or corrupt churchman does harm to the whole Church a dishonest trader does not in the same way harm the whole of his profession.

For further reading: Chapter 5, ' The Church and Religion ', in *English Life in the Middle Ages*, by L. F. Salzman, Oxford University Press, 1950; and, more fully, the chapters on the religious background and the clergy (especially 9–17, 22–3) in *Medieval Panorama*, by G. G. Coulton, Cambridge University Press, 1945. For a more detailed study see chapter 3, ' Madame Eglentyne, Chaucer's Prioress in Real Life ', in *Medieval People*, by Eileen Power, Pelican Books, 1951.

2. *The Faithful Clergy*

All his writings, the Prologue prominently among them, show Chaucer to have been both a fair-minded and a tolerant man. As a tolerant man he was ready to suffer not only fools gladly, but sinners, for he does not appear to have taken immediate exception to any of his fellows at Southwark:

> So hadde I spoken with hem everichon
> That I was of hir felaweshipe anon.   (31–2)

And as a fair-minded man he was ever ready to weigh up both sides of a question or of a person's character before pronouncing judgment on them. This is what Chaucer does in the Prologue where, as each pilgrim is presented to us in turn, we have the impression that Chaucer looks eagerly for something good in him or her to balance any faults or failings which he has also noted. As a result hardly any of the pilgrims emerge as wholly good or wholly bad, but as we shall see there are a few exceptions, some all the more damning for having no redeeming features at all, others so good that we feel that Chaucer was idealising a type to serve as an example to his contemporaries.

Of these latter the poor PARSON is the most obvious instance. In an age when so many members of the clergy were lax and selfish and neglectful of their duties, he stands out as almost unbelievably righteous and conscientious. Indeed, the only fault we can find is his lack of patience with obstinate sinners,

> Hym wolde he snybben sharply for the nonys,
> (523)

and even this is really a virtue in disguise. What Chaucer's aim in the Parson's portrait was we cannot know for certain, but its effect is the two-fold one of presenting a model of the good Christian shepherd and of drawing attention to the worst failings among contemporary parish priests of which this Parson is not guilty, such as using the dreaded penalty of excommunication upon poor parishioners who had failed to pay their tithes (486), or neglecting the parish in order to seek more profitable employment elsewhere (507–11).

The methods which Chaucer employs to serve this double purpose are both firm favourites of his: repetition and contrast. Certain key-words are repeated, like *good* (477, 520); *benygne* (483, 518); *clene, clennesse* (504, 506); *sheep, shepherde* (496, 504, 506, 508, 514). And effective contrasts are achieved, for example, between the Parson's material poverty and his spiritual wealth in 478–9:

> And was a *povre* Persoun of a Toun,
> But *riche* he was of hooly thoght and werk,

or between his own pastoral conscientiousness and the selfish greed of others (514). The result is a very Christlike figure, endowed with numerous Christian virtues (*devout, diligent, pacient, noble, clene, hooly, vertuous, discreet*), and twice we are directly reminded of Christ by mention of His name:

That Cristes gospel trewely wolde preche,   (481)
and

But Cristes loore and his apostles twelve
He taughte.   (527–8)

Yet as a person the Parson remains remote. Chaucer clearly intended this, for he tells us nothing about the man's clothes or equipment or his horse, and the only touch in the Prologue which reminds us that he really is meant to be a flesh-and-blood participant in the pilgrimage is the fact that he has a brother, the Plough-man, who is also there.

That such an idealised, and as a consequence rather unsubstantial, figure is rare among the Canterbury pilgrims is no doubt due to Chaucer's absorbing inter-est in people as individuals rather than as types, also to the difficulty of making such idealised figures come alive dramatically, and finally to the fact that Chaucer was much more at home among real people who had their share of faults and failings which he enjoyed describing with all the artistic means at his command. That is why the portraits of some of Chaucer's rogues are much more interesting than the Parson's; wicked people have always made more of a splash and hit the headlines more dramatically than the good ones. But Chaucer knew what he was doing. He needed such a virtuous cleric to offset the wholly disagreeable impression he was about to create with the last two pilgrims, the Summoner and the Pardoner, both thoroughly repulsive creatures, and he wanted to remind his audience of the important fact that though such good shepherds might be rare, the Christlike example remained.

The case is different with the first of the clerical pilgrims to whom the Prologue introduces us, the PRIORESS. This good lady is sometimes condemned outright as worldly, ambitious, and insensitive to the sufferings of others. But this is very harsh and largely undeserved criticism. There is no indication that she was neglectful of her responsible office as head of a convent, unless indeed her participation in a pilgrimage is to be taken as such in view of the fact that some of the Bishops of the time were strongly against nuns leaving their convents, even to go on a pilgrimage. But Chaucer says nothing of all this. What he does note is the Prioress's concern with good manners (127–36) and courtly etiquette (137–41), but these are largely explained by her probable background, for in the Middle Ages nuns were very commonly daughters of noble families brought up in polite society, and also by the esteem which her position in the Church inevitably accorded to her. Even the rather boisterous Host of the Tabard Inn addresses her with becoming respect:

' Cometh neer,' quod he, 'my lady Prioresse'. (839)

Her little indulgences, like displaying her forehead which should have been veiled (154–5), or carrying a few ornaments (158–62), are noted by the poet with genial tolerance, especially as the *Amor* of her motto (162) undoubtedly meant divine love, not earthly love, and particularly if we compare her little feminine failings with the Monk's monstrous self-indulgence.

On the other hand Chaucer credits his Prioress with several virtues which amply offset such weaknesses:

And al was conscience and tendre herte, (150)

where *conscience*, as also in 142, means 'feeling', or, perhaps more accurately, 'sensibility'. She was moderate in her speech (120) and her concern for small animals is a lovable trait in an age when cruelty was all too common (143–49). We might also note that the reference to the Prioress's French is no cheap gibe on Chaucer's part; the fact that she was content with the provincial French then still quite commonly in use in England, instead of going out of her way to emulate the French cultivated at court, is rather to her credit. That Chaucer, in describing the Prioress, uses words traditionally associated with descriptions of heroines of courtly romances and adventure tales, like ' ful symple and coy ' (119), or

> Hir nose tretys, hir eyen greye as glas,
> Hir mouth ful smal, and therto softe and reed
>
> (152–3)

is no criticism of the lady's character any more than might be an attempt on our part to describe a lady of our acquaintance by likening her face to that of a well-known film-star or television personality. On the contrary, there is a note of emphasis in the portrait achieved by the constant repetition of the emphatic *ful*, *wel*, and *so* in favourable contexts, and the threefold repetition of the very characteristic *ful semely*. The Prioress emerges as a conscientious nun who is also a lady, plainly over-anxious to do the right thing and prepared to err on the right side rather than offend against good manners or be false to her tender heart.

The Nun and Priest who accompany her are not described in the Prologue, but Chaucer draws another likable portrait in that of his Clerk, a poor Oxford scholar, also in Holy Orders, but too devoted to his books (294, 300) and learning (308) and study (303) to have as yet gained any material advancement (291–2), which is all to his credit.

3. *The Profiteering Clerics*

Chaucer's method of description by contrast is well illustrated by placing side by side the studious Clerk of Oxford and the hunting MONK. The one is in a few deft strokes featured as lean, hollow, threadbare, and his horse so thin that its protruding ribs make it look like a garden rake (287–90). The monk is *ful fat*, fond of *a fat swan*, well equipped on a berry-brown horse that suggests the same comfortable roundness as its master (200–7). The contrast is carried further, for while the Clerk loves to collect books and pore over them (293–6), the Monk disdains to

> studie and make hymselven wood,
> Upon a book in cloystre alwey to poure. (184–5)

Instead he collects horses and greyhounds (168, 190), for Chaucer takes pains to remind us several times of the Monk's absorbing passion for hunting (166, 177–8, 189, 191–2). Hunting monks were common enough throughout the Middle Ages so that Chaucer was probably as ready as other people to accept them in moderation as a necessary evil; but what he would not accept was the wholesale addiction to the sport to the exclusion of all else, including the basic demands made upon a monk by the rules of his Order. Hence the key to the Monk's portrait lies in the two lines

> Of prikyng and of huntyng for the hare
> Was *al* his lust, for *no* cost wolde he spare, (191–2)

with the metrical importance given to the emphatic *al* and *no* here underlined by printing them in italics. So when Chaucer claims that this ' manly man ' is fit to be an abbot (167), and that he is ' certeinly . . . a fair prelaat' (204), and that his opinions are worth something (183), he is of course not speaking in earnest, but with that tongue-in-the-cheek brand of humour, which is sometimes called ' irony ' in textbooks, and which Chaucer often uses to great effect. After all, it *was* a monk's duty to obey the rules of his Order however exacting (173–4), to study and toil (184–8), and not to spend time and money upon sport and finery (191–7) and, perhaps worst of all, to think such laxness very modern and up-to-date (175–6).

The Monk is not the worst offender among the erring clerics of the Canterbury pilgrimage, for at least his laxness and worldly interests do no direct harm to other people, although of course they don't do any good either to his Order or to his monastery. In the Pardoner's case the very profession is condemned as vicious, but Chaucer does not condemn the Monk for being a monk, rather for not properly being one.

Immediately after the Monk Chaucer introduces Hubert, the FRIAR, a member of one of the mendicant (or ' begging ') orders originally pledged to lives of service and poverty after the model of St. Francis of Assisi and the Spanish St. Dominic who had founded two of the four orders of friars in the thirteenth century. Hubert's case shows how little there was left by Chaucer's time of the selfless devotion of the original friars, and other records of the time prove that he was not exceptional. His is the longest portrait in the Prologue (62 lines); clearly his personality fascinated Chaucer. Again, as in the Parson's case, contemporary abuses are strongly criticised by the poet, but here they are the faults of an individual whose individuality (unlike the Parson's) is made memorable by small touches which Chaucer scatters here and there throughout the description: the Friar's white neck, for example (238), or his lisp (264), or his eyes twinkling when he sang to the harp

> as doon the sterres in the frosty nyght. (266–8)

Chaucer does not belittle either the man's unscrupulous dealings for personal profit in the name of religion—like his easy absolution from sin in exchange for ' a nice sum ' (223–4) or squeezing a farthing out of a destitute widow (253–5)—nor his self-indulgent habits. And yet Friar Hubert is not an unlikable fellow; he has an almost infectious gift of merriment, which Chaucer stresses in the first line of the portrait:

> A Frere ther was, a wantowne (= gay) and a merye,
> (208)

which is suggested also by the man's musical talents (235–7, 266), and which meets us unmistakably in Hubert's merry twinkling eyes (267–8). We might also note that, though the Friar gets mixed up in a quarrel with the Summoner later on in *The Canterbury Tales*, he keeps his temper and tells a good-humoured story directed at the other, while the repulsive Summoner gets angrier and more objectionable all the time.

The result of Chaucer's masterly portrait of the Friar is an uncompromising criticism of a devoted profession which has lost sight of its ideal, while yet not condemning the individual who isn't strong enough to withstand the tide of contemporary laxness and profiteering. As a friar Hubert is corrupt and depraved and without principles, but as an ordinary, fallible human being he is not, as Chaucer is at pains to make clear to us, without redeeming features.

But of the two remaining ' religious ' pilgrims even Chaucer, with all his tolerance and fair-mindedness, finds it impossible to say anything favourable. Significantly these are the last two of the pilgrims to be described, excepting the poet himself and the Host, and being birds of a feather they ride (and sing!) together (669–74). Both the SUMMONER and the PARDONER held offices which lent themselves to wholesale abuse, the one by accepting bribes from people whom he was meant to summon to appear in an ecclesiastical court (649–56), the other by allowing people to do penance and thus obtain pardon from their sins by paying him money, as well as by selling them any old rubbish claimed to be genuine sacred relics of the saints or apostles. Chaucer does not have to give many details of the frauds practised by these two ' noble ecclesiastics ' (708), for his contemporaries knew them only too well. But what he does tell is put over once again with the help of several devices which seem all too simple when we notice them, but which hide beneath their simplicity the art of a great poet. Like the *noble ecclesiaste* of the Pardoner just quoted, the Summoner is described in equally flattering and exaggerated terms which are all the more effective for implying exactly the opposite of what the words mean:

A bettre felawe sholde men noght fynde.   (648)

Chaucer, as we have already noted, is very fond of this device; did he not call the Monk ' a manly man, to been an abbot able' and Friar Hubert 'a worthy man' ? Equally effective is the playing with the key-words *curs* and *purs* in the Summoner's portrait, 653–62. Each word is used three times, and the word *purs* moves from the end of line 656, via the middle of line 657, to the beginning of line 658, becoming each time more emphatic; for it was his purse that would save the 'good fellow' (650, 653) who was being summoned for his sins, from the Archdeacon's punishment (*curs*) in the court.

The Pardoner is represented as a persuasive preacher who could 'wel affile (=make smooth) his tonge' (712), so that his profit would depend directly on this smooth-tonguedness. Again Chaucer creates just the right effect by a few skilful touches. The Pardoner's portrait depends to a great extent upon several striking similes which suggest smoothness, softness, and persuasiveness, like his ' heer as yelow as wex' and 'smothe . . . as . . . flex' (675–6), and the goatlike voice (688) which wheedled simple folk into buying his phoney relics. The very jingles which the Pardoner's smooth tongue employed in this ' feyned flaterye and japes' are echoed by Chaucer in a few alliterating phrases neatly inserted here and there into the passage which describes the Pardoner's activities:

a *p*ovre *p*erson	(702)
*m*oore *m*oneye	(703)
*f*eyned *f* laterye	(705)
the *p*erson and the *p*eple	(706)
*t*rewely to *t*ellen	(707)

For *w*el he *w*iste, whan that *s*ong was *s*onge.

(711)

In appearance these two pilgrims are very different: the Summoner loud-mouthed (673–4), more often than not drunk with blood-red wine which made his face fire-red (635, 624), covered with boils and pimples—a repulsive creature of whose ' visage children were aferd ' (628); the Pardoner all smooth and effeminate with his long, yellow hair (675–6), his stylish affectations (682–3), and his ' smal voys ' (688). Both men are referred to as *gentil* fellows (647, 669), a word which in its proper context was most precious to Chaucer (compare line 72), but which is here, by contrast, filled with the contempt which Chaucer obviously felt for both these depraved and corrupt ecclesiastics.

For further reading: Part III, chapters 1 and 2, ' Wandering Preachers and Friars ' and ' The Pardoners ', in *English Wayfaring Life in the Middle Ages* by J. J. Jusserand.

Questions:
1. One of Chaucer's methods of characterisation is to echo one pilgrim's portrait while describing some feature of another. What echoes of this kind can you find in the Friar's portrait? What is the purpose of each of these?
2. Which are the ecclesiastical abuses Chaucer singles out for specific condemnation? How many can you find in the clerical portraits and what further details can you add to Chaucer's from your own reading?

1. 'Sondry Folk'

Most of the lay pilgrims in the Prologue are neither very good nor very wicked, but they are all interesting. Chaucer wants us to accept them as a motley crowd

of sondry folk, by aventure yfalle,　　(25)

that is, come together by chance; but we soon realise that they are quite shrewdly chosen from a variety of trades and professions. For, as with the church pilgrims, Chaucer was interested in their professional background and activities as well as in their individual personalities. As a result we get numerous glimpses into the social and business life of the later fourteenth century. We see the medieval doctor in his surgery, the lawyers disputing in the courts, merchandise being bought and sold and shipped, a medieval marriage-ceremony by the church porch, and so forth. But we see even more than that, for we are looking through the observant, but by no means uncritical eyes of our poet-pilgrim, so that we also see the doctor making his little deal with the chemists supplying his patients, and the lawyers reeling off their unintelligible jargon of precedents from the time of William the Conqueror in order to impress their clients and get higher fees and a few more rich robes; and we see the ship's captain quietly rifling the merchandise entrusted to his care, and the same good lady married for the fifth time by the church porch and still going strong. Details like these bring the pilgrims more fully to life (and this of course applies also to the ecclesiastical pilgrims), for Chaucer realised that in order to make

C

them real and interesting for us we must be able to
picture them against their ordinary everyday background as well as in the holiday atmosphere of the
Canterbury pilgrimage. That we in the twentieth
century can learn from these portraits quite a lot about
life in the fourteenth is an incidental advantage which
probably never once occurred to Chaucer who was
busily writing to entertain his own contemporaries.

Chaucer was himself very much a man of practical
affairs with a sound respect for success in business or
professional practice. This respect speaks out of a
number of the lay portraits in the Prologue where we
see the pilgrims concerned no less aware of their own
profit and advantage than any astute professional or
business man of the twentieth century. Chaucer
accepts this as the natural order of secular business life
as readily as he condemned it among the church
pilgrims whose profession expressly forbade personal
gain.

The MANCIPLE (567–86), for example, is a highly
competent buyer of provisions for the college of
lawyers which employs him; indeed, we learn little
more about him from the poet than his business
efficiency. The sting, if there is any at all in this little
sketch, is directed rather against the lawyers, who
employ him, for being outwitted, despite all their
cleverness, by ' swich a lewed (= uneducated) mannes
wit ' (574). The Manciple caps the lot for sheer
business acumen (586) and the merchants who sell to
him as well (569), so that Chaucer is understandably
inclined to applaud him.

The SERGEANT OF THE LAW (309–330) and the
DOCTOR (411–444) impress Chaucer similarly as

thoroughly successful practitioners in their respective professions, even though there is a hint or two of not entirely scrupulous dealings. Of this Chaucer is rightly critical, but what he appears to dislike even more is hypocrisy, that is pretending to be something one isn't. Both men are condemned for this: the Lawyer for his pompous officiousness, for pretending that he was 'bisier than he was' (321-2); and the Doctor for claiming to know everything about medicine (419-24), which makes Chaucer poke fun at him in mock-serious words which are deliberately meant to invite comparison with the worthy Knight:

He was a verray, parfit praktisour. (422, compare 72)

On the other hand, Chaucer again gives credit where it is due. Both men are well-read in their professions —a fact which would impress Chaucer who was himself very fond of reading;—the Lawyer is as unassuming in his *hoomly* clothes for the pilgrimage which require no long description (328-30) as the Doctor is moderate in his personal habits (435). That the Doctor is very fond of acquiring money but reluctant to spend it Chaucer notes with a good-humoured dig (441-4), but the fact that he was going on a pilgrimage while sharing with most doctors of the time a reputation for not believing in God is passed over by the poet without any further comment at all (438).

We picked these three pilgrims out of the middle of the Prologue to show how Chaucer reacted to men who were successful in secular pursuits. But the poet of course quite properly begins with the KNIGHT,

because social (or class) distinctions were quite rigidly
defined in Chaucer's day and because the audience for
whom Chaucer was writing would expect it like that.
That the Knight is also the first to tell a tale is probably
more due to design on the Host's part than to accident
(842–58). Among the secular pilgrims present the
Knight occupies first place, corresponding to the
Lady Prioress, as head of a convent, among the
ecclesiastics, but the closest counterpart to the Knight
among the latter is not the Prioress, despite her
consciousness of rank and ' cheere of court ', but the
poor Parson. Both portraits are idealised, but the
Knight becomes a more substantial creature than the
priest because we see him on his horse and are told
enough about his *bismotered* clothes to picture him
hurrying straight from his latest voyage to give thanks
at St. Thomas's shrine. Also, although the list of the
Knight's campaigns reads rather like a conventional
travel brochure, some of the places are sufficiently
distinctive for Chaucer's contemporaries to have
regarded this particular Knight as a distinct individual,
perhaps even made him recognisable as some contemporary champion. On the other hand, like the
Parson, the Knight is presented to us as a thoroughly
virtuous man and a model of knighthood (which many
fourteenth-century knights were not) who is repeatedly
described as *worthy* and credited with almost as many
virtues as the Christlike priest (see: 45–6, 50, 68–9, 72,
850–2). And as the Parson grows in virtue by being
innocent of all the vices and abuses Chaucer enumerates, so the Knight's character gains by contrast with
the help of two memorable lines in which the poet
uses four negatives to hammer home the point:

He *nevere* yet *no* vileynye *ne* sayde
In al his lyf unto *no* maner wight.   (70–1)

The second line, which further affirms the Knight's *life-
long* virtuousness, will remind us of another important
line which we have already met, although it occurs
later in the Prologue; for when the Monk's passionate
devotion to hunting is described, Chaucer deliberately
echoes the good Knight, thus doubling the effectiveness, when we come to it, of the line

Was *al* his lust, for *no* cost wolde he spare. (192)

Such a knight as Chaucer here describes was no
doubt as rare in the late fourteenth century as was the
saintly parish priest. The poet's purpose was thus
much the same in both cases: to place before his
audience ideals of which his age was losing sight.
On the one hand he places the faithful shepherd as an
example to a corrupt clergy, on the other he places the
true gentleman as a model for all those who were
forgetting that true *worthynesse* was a matter not of
clothes and riches and fine horses, but of honesty,
modesty, integrity, in short: of character.

It soon becomes obvious that most of the other
pilgrims are not particularly concerned about the
worthynesse or *gentilesse* which the Knights stands for,
except for the Squire and the Franklin. The former is
the Knight's son (79) and as befits his background is
himself an apprentice knight. But he is also a young
man eager for his lady's favour (88), so that the
portrait Chaucer paints for us is a skilful blend of
youthfulness, chivalry in the making, and thoughts of
music and love. Each of these aspects of the Squire's

personality has its own series of telling words and phrases, all neatly intertwined and made even more effective by vivid word-pictures like

He was as fressh as is the month of May   (92)

or

He sleep namoore than doth a nyghtyngale.   (98)

That this young man should be *curteis* and *lowely* (99) we would expect from one whose father ' loved . . . curteisie ' (45–6) and was, moreover, ' as meeke as is a mayde ' (69).

The FRANKLIN'S concern with *gentilesse* becomes really apparent only when his turn arrives to tell a story much later in *The Canterbury Tales*, but from the Prologue we see that it derives from his position as ' a worthy vavasour ' (360), a country gentleman of considerable importance in his county (355–6, 359) who very fittingly had as his travelling companion another man of importance, the Sergeant of the Law (331), and who probably qualified as next in rank to the Knight among the secular pilgrims. His portrait in the Prologue is a masterpiece of over-emphasis, for the Franklin's one enormous failing is a love of food which Chaucer is at great pains to drive home by devoting twenty-one lines of the Franklin's thirty to a description of the latter's ever-ready table and the delights to be found on it. As for the rest, we catch just enough glimpses of this portly gentleman to be impressed by the contrast of colours Chaucer draws between the ruddy face and the whiteness of beard and silken purse, while in his house, we are reminded, ' it snewed . . . of mete and drynke ' (345). Such touches are important for us to note, for it is on carefully chosen details of this kind that Chaucer's portraits so often rely.

The remaining pilgrims, apart from the poet himself, are all skilled in some trade or craft, including the Wife of Bath who is expert at *clooth-makyng* (447) and the Reeve who, although now an administrator of a large estate, was trained as a carpenter (613–4). Of these craftsmen and tradesmen Chaucer bundles the FIVE GILDSMEN together as belonging to some common social or religious fraternity (361–4). But we don't meet them as individuals beyond an impression that their wealth and fine array and social importance are all very recent (365–72), and this impression is strengthened both by the reference to the snobbish ambitions of their wives (374–8) and by the fact that the Gildsmen have brought a cook along with them on the pilgrimage, probably as much to impress their neighbours as to provide for their meals (379).

The COOK's portrait is the shortest in the Prologue (nine lines: 379–87), if we exclude the Nun and Nun's Priest who are only just mentioned, but when the Cook comes to begin his story later in *The Canterbury Tales* we realise that Chaucer has been saving up more details. It is only then that we learn that the Cook's name is Roger, for example, and that he is quite a lad, of which the Prologue gives us just a hint in the line

Wel koude he knowe a draughte of Londoun ale.

(382)

Apart from this the Prologue enlarges a little on the Cook's professional skill and mentions the unfortunate sore on his shin which the poet obviously meant to be sufficiently noticeable to get such special mention.

In the portraits of the SHIPMAN (388–410), which follows the Cook's, and of the MERCHANT (270–84) somewhat earlier, Chaucer turns our attention to two men whose professions were of national importance in Chaucer's time no less than at other periods of British history. The merchants were a powerful class and quite aware of it; hence the distinctive clothes and pompous bearing of Chaucer's fork-bearded Merchant, which hide the fact that for all his doubtful dealings he was in debt (278–82). If we recall the *worthy* Knight then the double reference to the Merchant as 'a worthy man' must again be taken with a large Chaucerian dose of salt (279, 283). In a similar way the Shipman is referred to as

>   certainly he was a good felawe,   (395)

and in some ways he no doubt was, for the tradition of English seafaring is worthily enough represented in one who

> knew alle the havenes, as they were,
> Fro Gootlond to the cape of Fynystere,
> And every cryke in Britaigne and in Spayne,
>
>   (407–9)

and who had brought his 'Maudelayne' safely through many a tempest (406). Once again Chaucer readily applauds professional skill. On the other hand, this seadog from Dartmouth has his shady sides and this sketch of him does not ignore them (396–400), any more than in the case of the Merchant. Both portraits are fine examples of just how much detail of appearance and character and professional skill Chaucer can pack into less than two dozen lines of verse.

Another pair we might consider together are the
MILLER and the REEVE, for as it turns out they get
involved in a quarrel almost as soon as the pilgrimage
begins, and their dislike of each other is hinted at by
the distance they keep: the Miller leads the pilgrims
out of town with his bagpipe (565–6), while the Reeve
always rides at the end (622). In appearance, too, they
are made to contrast sharply, for everything about the
Miller is big and uncouth while the Reeve is long and
thin. The very method of description Chaucer employs
stresses the contrast further: the Miller's sketch
devotes only four of twenty-two lines to the man's
character (560–3), the rest describes his appearance
with the help of a number of words denoting bigness
(*stout, byg, brawn, brood, thikke, wyde, greet*), some apt
similes like the two references to a sow (552, 556) or

His mouth as greet was as a greet forneys,   (559)

and several rollicking phrases like *a stout carl* (545) or
a thicke knarre (549). The Reeve's portrait, on the
other hand, concentrates more than twice as much on
the man's character and business methods as on his
appearance. And yet the few lines 587–92 give a good
picture of the man with the help of a few carefully
chosen phrases: *a sclendre colerik man* (587), *his top was
dokked* (590), and the line

Ful longe were his legges and ful lene   (591)

where all the *l*'s combine into a strong impression of
elongation, once more briefly echoed by the *long
surcote* of line 617. Both men are adept at dishonest
practices, mentioned in similar phrases, for in this
respect Chaucer makes them very alike:

Miller: Wel koude he stelen corn and tollen thries
(562)
Reeve: Wel koude he kepe a gerner and a bynne . . .
(593)
His lord wel koude he plesen subtilly. (610)

Again we are made to admire the skill with which Chaucer can bring home to us in a few well-chosen lines this striking similarity in two so dissimilar figures.

Another masterly portrait, perhaps the most famous of all, is that of the only woman among the secular pilgrims, the WIFE OF BATH, who really comes from *biside Bathe*, that is from the parish of St. Michael's just outside the old city itself. Her portrait is like the Squire's in that it mingles the salient features into a composite picture rather than enumerates them one after the other as in the case, for example, of the Shipman. In the Wife's case the main features are: (1) her appearance and clothes, all very big and conspicuous; (2) her character; and (3) her skill and experience, whether in cloth-making, love and marriage, or pilgrimages. In every sense Chaucer makes her into an overwhelming personality, very different from the other female character already described, the Prioress. The one is as loud in speech and laughter as in her clothes (474, 453-7), and easily ' out of alle charitee' (452) when crossed; the Prioress is modest in speech and manner and 'so charitable' (143). One detail of the Wife's description illustrates how Chaucer intended to link the Prologue to the remainder of *The Canterbury Tales*; and this is her deafness (446). For we learn much later in the work that in a fight with her fifth husband the Wife received a blow on the head which caused her to be *somdel deef*.

The reference to the Wife's many pilgrimages is Chaucer's way of further drawing attention to the woman's buoyant, pleasure-loving disposition; perhaps he also believed with many of his contemporaries that the gap between the Wife's front teeth (468) was proverbially a sign of a pleasure-loving and much-travelled person. That we are not to take these many pilgrimages of hers as indications of a particularly earnest religious temperament is further made clear by other hints, such as the Wife's love of good company (474) which she was very likely to find on pilgrimages, her Sunday-best attire, and the fact that she was as interested in what happened on her journeys as in their destinations (467). In short, in this big, loud, jolly woman from Bath Chaucer has given us a unique Englishwoman of six centuries ago who remains one of the great creations of our literature.

Two lay pilgrims remain who help to balance to some extent the wholly unfavourable impressions of the profligate Summoner and Pardoner among the churchmen by having nothing critical said about them at all. Neither tells a tale so that we don't meet them further. One, the PLOUGHMAN, is the brother of the Christlike Parson, and is himself a good Christian and a conscientious worker; indeed, the words *swynkere*, 'worker', and *swynk*, 'work', as it were enclose the little sketch Chaucer draws for us (531, 540). In Chaucer's time there was unrest and discontent among the country folk; workers were few after the ravages of pestilence, and their lives were hard and unrewarding. This unrest led in 1381 (only a few years, remem-

ber, before the Prologue was written) to the Peasants'
Revolt in which the land-workers tried hard, but
without success, to better their living and working
conditions. Chaucer's whole nature would incline
sympathetically to the poor and oppressed, but he was
intelligent enough to realise that the country must
have the harvests on which its food and livelihood
depended, and that therefore men must be found to till
the soil and be prepared to work hard on the land even
under the primitive conditions then prevailing. Hence
the Ploughman's portrait, parallel to the Parson's, is
something of an appeal for good honest toil and the
contentment to be derived from it:

> A trewe swynkere and a good was he,
> Lyvynge in pees and parfit charitee.   (531–2)

It is no accident that Parson and Ploughman are
brothers and are described one after the other.

Many discontented peasants and ploughmen of the
later fourteenth century had abandoned altogether the
hard but honest life of this Ploughman and taken
instead to the highways and forests of England, which
were then much more extensive than now, to form
bands of robbers and outlaws, by no means always as
honourable in their methods as Robin Hood and his
men. Chaucer's YEOMAN (101–17) at once reminds us
of Robin Hood, both in appearance and by his skill in
archery and woodcraft, but there is nothing of the
outlaw about him. He remains at best a neutral
character for us, as Chaucer says nothing about him
beyond his skill and appearance. The Yeoman is a
forester by trade, seemingly a model of his craft, but
he goes on the pilgrimage in attendance upon the

Knight, for it was then customary for a Knight to travel thus attended. Whether Chaucer intended to elaborate the Yeoman later in *The Canterbury Tales* into a more distinctive and interesting personality, as he does with the Cook, we shall of course never know; in the portrait itself there is no hint.

The remainder of the Prologue is devoted to a narrative of events leading to the beginning of the pilgrimage proper, an outline of the scheme of story-telling devised by the Host of the Tabard Inn, a few glimpses of the POET CHAUCER himself as one of the twenty-nine pilgrims, and a slightly fuller description of the HOST whom we get to know later as Harry Bailey. Both in the description of him and in his own words (751–83) the key-words are *myrie* and *myrthe*; obviously Harry Bailey was a jolly man, whose chief idea was to make the pilgrimage itself a great success as entertainment (*myrthe, ese, confort, disport*) with not a little profit to himself thrown in. As master of cere-monies he dominates the stage from the end of the Prologue onwards, and he is large and imposing enough to do this very impressively. With such a man in charge of such a motley assembly anything might happen on the road to Canterbury, and a lot of things do!

For further reading: The chapters on secular life in Salzman's *English Life in the Middle Ages* (especially chapters 2–4, 10–12) and in Coulton's *Medieval Panorama* (especially chapters 6–7, 24–7, 33–4).

Questions:
1. In discussing some of the portraits (e.g. the Knight, Parson, etc.) we noted Chaucer's use of key-

words and key-phrases. Which words do you think play a similar role in the portraits of (a) the Clerk; (b) the Miller; (c) the Host?

2. Analyse the Wife of Bath's portrait and explain what each point adds to our general impression.

3. What justification is there for regarding the following lines as keys to the characters referred to?

(a) And al was conscience and tendre herte —Prioress,
(b) Of his complexioun he was sangwyn—Franklin,
(c) A trewe swynkere and a good was he—

Ploughman.

2. *The Prologue as a Source of Knowledge*

The Prologue is a poem, a work of art, and we must not be tempted either to treat it as a piece of fourteenth-century history, or to regard every pilgrim mentioned as modelled on a real person or every detail about the pilgrims as accurate contemporary records. Nevertheless, it is a source of much interesting information. We can learn a lot from it, and some of it will help us to understand Chaucer's pilgrims even better and to form a better picture of the poet's art.

Chaucer's Doctor of Medicine, for example, we are told, injects a good deal of *astronomye* (what we would now call ' astrology ') into his medical practice by seeing first whether the stars are in favourable positions before carrying out an operation on a patient or prescribing some other treatment (415–18). Or the Yeoman carries an image of St. Christopher, patron of foresters, on his chest (115). Such details are not meant to single out the respective pilgrims as particularly superstitious or brand the doctor as a quack, for belief in the controlling influence of the stars on the affairs of men or in the protective powers of the saints was common then, and as we saw, it is upon such innocent beliefs that men like the Pardoner were trading. On the other hand the not inconsiderable star-lore of the Middle Ages was often used for purposes where even to-day we might still use astronomy, as in the Shipman's craft (401–4).

Of a different kind are the many details of contemporary clothing which Chaucer describes, of which there must have been a rich and colourful variety in the thirteen-eighties. Several of the pilgrims are conspicuously armed, others carry small items of equipment, like a silken purse or a pouch or a pair of sharp spurs or a musical instrument. Again Chaucer can use details of this kind not only to describe his pilgrims' appearance, but to throw further light on their characters. Thus the Wife of Bath, with her ambition to be the first *wif* in her parish, becomes even more amusingly provincial when we read of her heavy Sunday-best *coverchiefs* (453–5) which were at least twenty years out of fashion by the time Chaucer was writing.

We are told much of contemporary food and although some of the dishes are no doubt familiar, others sound decidedly strange to us. And there is ample reference to wine and ale to prove their popularity in the fourteenth century. It is worth noting that references to food or drink or to both play their part in at least ten of the twenty-nine portraits.

Of contemporary crafts, trades, and professions, being so variously represented, we gain much valuable detail which is again, in many cases, used directly to help characterise the pilgrims. Chaucer's choice of pilgrims takes us into medieval towns as well as country places; only the royal court and the higher nobility are not represented as they would not join a common pilgrimage then any more than our sovereign would be expected to join a popular coach outing to Blackpool. The glimpses we have of the Tabard Inn, for example, reveal what would even to-day be quite a large hotel, capable of accommodating twenty-nine visitors *atte beste* (29), providing for them ample food and drink, and finding stabling for their horses. The master of such a place was indeed fit

> for to han been a marchal in an halle.   (752)

An incidental reference to the *table dormant* which always stood *redy covered* (353-4) in the Franklin's house helps to emphasise further that gentleman's love of food and hospitality by stressing that his table was permanently fixed in his hall. The more common medieval practice was to use trestle tables which could be removed to make more space in what would be the main room of a house.

Sometimes the picturesque similes which Chaucer uses to elaborate a point reveal glimpses of fourteenth-century life; they also show how much closer town and country were at that time: there are word-pictures involving, for example, animals and flowers, or tools and instruments used on the land, all of which would be perfectly familiar even to the most courtly members of Chaucer's audience in the heart of London. Moreover, details of country pursuits like forestry or farming show that Chaucer himself was as much at home in the country as among the trades and professions of the town. Not many poets could claim the same to-day. It was Chaucer's good fortune that he was able to bring to his poetry the experience of a very varied, interesting, and observant active life.

For further reading: A handy introduction to Chaucer's background is *Introducing Chaucer* by N. G. Brett-James, London, 1949. *Chaucer and his England* by G. G. Coulton, 7th edition, London 1946, is valuable for both beginners and more advanced students. See also Parts I and II of Jusserand's *English Wayfaring Life in the Middle Ages*, and *Chaucer and the Mediaeval Sciences* by W. C. Curry, New York and London, 1926.

Questions:
1. What have you learnt from the Prologue of EITHER (a) dress OR (b) food and drink in fourteenth-century England? What use does Chaucer make of EITHER (a) OR (b) as means of characterisation?
2. What have you learnt from the Prologue about travelling in the fourteenth century? How relevant are these details to the Prologue as a poem?

D

IV. Chaucer's Art

1. *Language and Metre*

It is nearly six hundred years since the Prologue to *The Canterbury Tales* was written so that we need not be surprised to find Chaucer's English rather different from ours. But often the differences are purely on the surface, so that a little re-arranging of spelling or of the order of a sentence may be all we need to get perfectly good sense. For instance, the line

to telle yow al the condicioun (38)

is easily recognised as the modern English

to tell you all the condition,

but if it were printed like this, the metre of Chaucer's line would be spoilt, as this depends on stressing words or syllables which we might not stress to-day:

to téll-e yów ál the condícióun,

and of pronouncing the *e* in the final syllables of many words, as in *telle*, where to-day we either have no *e* left at all or don't pronounce it any more, as in:

she hadd-e pass-ed many a straung-e strem (464)
she had passed many a strange stream.

The secret of reading Chaucer's verse aright is to discover, mainly by trial and error, when and when not to pronounce these *e*'s. Sometimes the text helps. For example, in the edition from which all our quotations have been copied, lines 90 and 92 distinguish between *fresshe* and *fressh*, where the first is plural and must be read with two syllables:

Al ful of fresshe floures, whyte and reede, (90)

He was as fressh as is the month of May. (92)

Practice will make perfect; so make a point of reading Chaucer's verse out aloud, putting five stresses into each line, and you will learn to master and thoroughly enjoy the smooth flow of his poetry.

There are of course some difficulties in Chaucer's language which we must face. They are mainly to do with vocabulary and are of two kinds. First of all we have words which are completely strange to us because the English language had no further use for them so that they have disappeared. Such words may prevent our understanding a passage of Chaucer until we have looked them up in our glossary, which is the obvious remedy. For example:

This worthy lymytour was cleped Huberd.

(269)

Both *lymytour* and *cleped* are strange words, although we might guess that Huberd is the same as Hubert so that *cleped* looks as if it meant ' named ' or ' called ', which it does indeed mean. And *lymytour*, when looked up in the glossary and found to mean ' a friar licenced to beg within a definite limit ', makes Chaucer's meaning clear enough. Unfamiliar words, then, may cause us a little trouble, but not misunderstanding.

This is the danger with the second type of words, those which look familiar but are used by the poet in different senses from those they have to-day. Here we must be on our guard so as not to miss or misinterpret Chaucer's meaning. Here are four important examples:

(1) *vileynye*: as the ' villeins ' were a separate social

class of farm labourers, this word conveyed a social rather than a moral meaning; it means vulgarity rather than immorality. Hence the line

> He nevere yet no vileynye ne sayde   (70)

means that the Knight was never guilty of discourteous, coarse, or rude speech unbecoming of his rank and profession of knighthood. The word is used similarly in 726 and 740.

(2) *conscience*: in 142 and 150 Chaucer's use of the word refers to the Prioress's 'feeling' or 'sensibility', but in 398 there is much more of the modern meaning,

> Of nyce conscience took he no keep;

the Shipman was troubled neither by tender feelings nor by scruples of conscience.

(3) *solempne*: when Friar Hubert is referred to as 'a ful solempne man' (209) we are liable to get a very wrong impression of this merry fellow with his twinkling eyes, for the modern word 'solemn' fits in neither with the words 'a wantowne and a merye' of the preceding line nor with the character of the Friar as a whole. Hence we must accept the earlier meaning of 'festive' here, which is what the word meant in Latin where it originally came from, suggesting in this context the Friar's jovial and sociable disposition. In another context, however, the word may already be much closer to our modern meaning; when it comes to the Merchant, for instance, the poet tells us that

> his resons he spak ful solempnely,   (274)

that is every word was a 'feast', a 'special occasion', so that we might render *solempnely* as 'pompously', or

' impressively ', or ' importantly '. In much the same way the word is used in the line

> Of a solempne and a greet fraternitee   (364)

to which the Five Gildsmen belong.

(4) *honest*:

> It is nat honest, it may nat avaunce,
> For to deelen with no swich poraille,   (246–7)

says Chaucer of the Friar. But Friar Hubert was never much troubled by questions of honesty, so that we should get a very wrong idea of his motives if we took this word in its modern sense. The meaning must be ' honourable, respectable ', it was not ' the thing done ' to associate with such poor folk as lepers or beggars, quite apart from the lack of profit in such quarters.

From these examples the need for care is obvious when reading Chaucer's poetry. We shall miss much of Chaucer's intention and a great deal of his humour unless we make a point of looking out for words which *seem* the same as their modern English descendants, but which don't quite fit into the context with their modern meanings.

Just as there are differences in appearance and meaning between Chaucer's words and ours to-day, so there are differences in arrangement, or syntax. These differences need not cause us any trouble if we read the text carefully. A few examples will show this. In lines like

> In al this world *ne* was ther *noon* hym lik,   (412)

> *No* berd hadde he, *ne nevere* sholde have,   (689)

the doubled or trebled negatives (of which Chaucer is
very fond) do not obscure the poet's meaning; they
help to emphasise it. Sometimes Chaucer uses a verb
without a subject where modern usage requires one,
as in

> *Bifil* that in that seson on a day;   (19)

at other times a number of clauses may be strung
together without a verb, for example:

> and on hir heed an hat
> As brood as is a bokeler or a targe;
> A foot-mantel aboute hir hipes large,
> And on hir feet a paire of spores sharpe. (470–3)

A construction which might at first look rather odd
to us is used in 423–4:

> The cause yknowe, and of his harm the roote,
> Anon he yaf . . .

but this is not without parallels in modern English.
Chaucer's word-order is sometimes different from ours
either because he was following normal fourteenth-
century practice, or else because he wished to create a
particular poetic effect, or simply for reasons of rhyme.
In no case should we have any difficulty in understanding his meaning:

> At mortal batailles hadde he been fiftene,   (61)

> In al this world ne was ther noon hym lik,   (412)

> A good man was ther of religioun.   (477)

For further reading: Chapter 6, ' Chaucer's Language
and Versification ', in *A Chaucer Handbook* by R. D.

French. Chapter 11, ' How Middle English was spelt and how it sounded,' in *Early English* by J. W. Clark, London, 1957, is much more technical; at the end of the chapter there is a phonetic transcription of lines 1–18 of the Prologue. A useful introduction to the history of the English language as a whole is *The Spell of Words* by John and Joan Levitt, London, 1959.

Questions:

1. Select and comment on any six words from the Prologue, not discussed in the text, which have developed different meanings since Chaucer's time.

2. Select and explain any six words from the Prologue which are no longer part of the language. Why do you think they fell into disuse?

3. Attempt a modern rendering in heroic couplets of lines 193–204 of the Prologue, or of any other passage of similar length.

2. *Chaucer's Style*

A writer's style is the way in which he chooses and uses his words to convey what he wants to say, and Chaucer, like other poets, has his own mannerisms of expression and arrangement which make his poetry distinct from that of other writers. Certain features of Chaucer's style, like his conversational ease or the use of repetition, no doubt derive from the fact that Chaucer wrote much of his poetry in the first place for recitation to a cultured, courtly audience.[1] It will

---

[1] There is a fine fourteenth-century picture in a manuscript in Corpus Christi College, Cambridge, which shows Chaucer reading his poetry to a courtly audience. This is reproduced on page 153 of Salzman's *English Life in the Middle Ages*.

help us to understand and appreciate Chaucer's style more fully if we keep this fact in mind.

At the simplest level we find certain common words and phrases of which Chaucer is very fond. Often he probably hardly noticed this, as when he is using, for example, the word *faire* as a useful descriptive adjective in many places with no particular force attached to it:

> Wel semed ech of hem a fair burgeys,   (369)

> A fairer burgeys is ther noon in Chepe.   (754)

Other expressions of which Chaucer is very fond are phrases of the type ' wel koude he ', ' wel knew he ', ' ful pacient ', ' ful byg ', where the short *wel* and *ful* merely help the metre of the line. But even such humble words as *wel* and *ful* can be made to carry much greater weight, as in the Prioress's portrait where their constant repetition and the stress they receive in several lines create that effect of emphasis and eagerness which we noted on page 18.

To keep the metre of a line going properly Chaucer not only uses such short words as *wel* and *ful*, but sometimes inserts little phrases, often called ' tags ', which may add little or nothing at all to the meaning but help the line to scan. One soon comes to recognise some of these tags as very characteristic of Chaucer, and as they are often put in the first person, they help every now and then to establish a direct link between poet and reader which in turn increases one's pleasure in the poetry. In the Prologue they can therefore act as useful reminders that it is in fact the poet-pilgrim Chaucer who is describing his fellows to us:

Of twenty yeer of age he was, *I gesse*,   (82)

Ful fetys was hir cloke, *as I was war*,   (157)

But greet harm was it, *as it thoughte me*,   (385)

Of Northfolk was this Reve *of which I telle*.   (619)

But at other times no particular importance need be attached to them:

But, *sooth to seyn*, I noot how men hym calle. (284)

There is a conversational ring about such phrases which points to another important characteristic of Chaucer's style, namely, an easy flow of language in which the manner of ordinary conversation seems quite without effort transformed into poetry. Of course, it is not as effortless as it seems and we may be sure that Chaucer had to work very hard to achieve an effect which satisfied him, and it took him many years to do it. Chaucer's earlier poems, like the elegy which he wrote in 1369–70 on the death of John of Gaunt's wife, *The Book of the Duchess*, show a less accomplished verse, although here and there the later mastery is foreshadowed. The choice of the heroic couplet as the verse form of the Prologue and most of *The Canterbury Tales* helped greatly in the attainment of this mastery, because the lines have a more comfortable length than the shorter lines of *The Book of the Duchess* or *The House of Fame*, another early poem. Also, the couplets ensure a steady procession of different rhymes which is easier to sustain without artificiality or monotony than is sometimes the case with more elaborate stanza forms such as Chaucer uses in two of his other major works, *The Parliament of Fowls* and *Troilus and Criseyde*. There are several useful points for us to note here in connection with Chaucer's conversational style:

In the first place, Chaucer's tags themselves mirror some of the discursiveness and even untidiness which seems to have been a mark of conversational English in the fourteenth as much as in the twentieth century. Where we might pepper our speech with words like ' sure ' or ' sort of ' Chaucer uses ' sikerly ' or ' trewely to tellen ' and the like. Then he adds further to this colloquial tone by making use quite often of common turns of speech, popular idioms, proverbial sayings, even slang, as well as relying very largely on plain, ordinary words such as one was most likely to have heard on a fourteenth-century Kentish highway. Lines like these, for instance, seem to be lifted straight from the plain, conversational English of Chaucer's time into the verse of the Prologue:

> So hadde I spoken with hem everichon
> That I was of hir felaweshipe anon,
> And made forward erly for to ryse,
> To take oure wey ther as I yow devyse.   (31–4)

> A not heed hadde he, with a broun visage.   (109)

> He knew the tavernes wel in every toun.   (240)

> His studie was but litel on the Bible.   (438)

> A fewe termes hadde he, two or thre,
> That he had lerned out of som decree—
> No wonder is, he herde it al the day.   (639–41)

> And if he foond owher a good felawe.   (653)

Sometimes a picturesque popular phrase is used, as

when the Monk pooh-poohs the rules of his Order
which did not appeal to him:

> He yaf nat of that text a pulled hen, (177)

> But thilke text heeld he nat worth an oystre;
> (182)

or a contemporary proverb:

> And yet he hadde a thombe of gold, pardee,
> (563)

where the final *pardee* adds still further to the colloquial
effect.

Next we should note that although Chaucer mostly
uses very ordinary words, he chooses them carefully
so that the order in which they are arranged and the
patterns of sound which they create when read aloud
should be satisfying to the ear and enhance our enjoyment. For example, the seemingly very ordinary
description of the Cook's skill—

> He koude rooste, and sethe, and broille, and frye,
> (383)

is made very effective because the variety of vowel
sounds and diphthongs (each main word has a different
one) underlines the variety of cooking techniques
enumerated, while the length of these sounds in
rooste, sethe, broille, frye (and all these were long sounds
in Chaucer's time too) coupled with the repeated *and*
make the catalogue of accomplishments seem longer
than it really is.

Another time a slight re-arranging of very common
words can turn an ordinary sentence into one of greater
emphasis and consequent poetic effectiveness, as in this

line where in Chaucer's time as in our own the more common word order would reverse the positions of the first and third words:

> God loved he best with al his hoole herte,   (533)

—how much more effective than if Chaucer had written:

> He loved God best with al his hoole herte.

And notice also how the emphatic *God* at the opening of the line is balanced by the duplicated *al* and *hoole* in the second half. One of these would have done; the two together drive home the Ploughman's whole-hearted love of God still more forcibly.

A combination of short words can have an emphatic hammering effect, as in the line just quoted, or else produce a light, tripping or dancing effect where the sense requires it. This is because in such lines the basic five-beat rhythm is at its most obvious. Such effects we get, for example, in the portrait of the lively young Squire:

> He was as fressh as is the month of May,   (92)

or when the Miller's bagpipe plays the company on its way:

> And therwithal he broghte us out of towne.   (566)

On the other hand, longer ' dictionary ' words tend to slow down the verse and to add solemnity or pompousness to the occasion or character described, very appropriately so, for example, in the case of the Lawyer:

Discreet he was and of greet *reverence*—
He seemed swich, his wordes weren so wise.
Justice he was ful often in *assise*,
By *patente* and by *pleyn commissioun.*
For his *science* and for his heigh *renoun*,
Of fees and robes hadde he many oon.
So greet a *purchasour* was nowher noon:
All was *fee symple* to hym in *effect*;
His *purchasyng* myghte nat been *infect*.   (312–20)

Similarly, the learned Doctor is ' a verray, parfit praktisour ' (422) in Chaucer's mock-serious description and we are given an impressive list of his medical reading, which gave the poet a welcome opportunity to show off his own wide reading which he enjoyed doing. And the fact that the Doctor ate little and was what we might to-day call ' vitamin-conscious ' is expressed with the help of more learned-looking words which further underline the Doctor's self-importance and extravagant claims:

Of his diete *mesurable* was he,
For it was of no *superfluitee*,
But of greet *norissyng* and *digestible*.   (435–7)

Sometimes Chaucer chooses words which alliterate to make a line more effective:

Ful *b*yg he was of *b*rawn, and eek of *b*ones,   (546)

Ful *l*onge were his *l*egges and ful *l*ene,   (591)

With scalled *b*rowes *b*lake and piled *b*erd.   (627)

Or else he may pick words whose sounds add force to their descriptive meaning, like *knarre*, ' sturdy fellow ',

(549) or *knobbes*, ' pimples ', (633) where the *k* was still pronounced in Chaucer's time.

Finally, Chaucer's style embraces the use of a number of poetic devices, such as figures of speech or images which make a point or a character more vivid by implied or expressed comparison with something else. The Middle Ages particularly admired in a writer's work what they called ' the colours of rhetoric ', by which they meant all the arts and devices which a writer would use to vary and elaborate his use of words. There is not a character among the Canterbury pilgrims whose description is not enlivened in several ways by Chaucer's use of such stylistic devices. It may be by a straightforward comparison:

> And of his port as meeke as is a mayde, (69)
>
> His nekke whit was as the flour-de-lys, (238)
>
> As brood as is a bokeler or a targe, (471)
>
> As greet as it were for an ale-stake. (667)

Or it may be by a poetic image more subtly woven into the text as when the Parson and his parishioners become shepherd and sheep; or when, as we saw on page 30, the Franklin's daisy-white beard and milk-white purse are further enhanced, as well as his love of food further emphasised, by

> It snewed in his hous of mete and drynke; (345)

or when the Summoner's horrible face is comically described as ' a fyr-reed cherubynnes face ' (624).

Sometimes Chaucer deliberately repeats an idea in succeeding lines, not only for emphasis, but in order to introduce some subtle twist which comes as a surprise to the reader, as when the Friar's pleasant manner of hearing confession and granting absolution is suddenly explained, after the second reference, in terms of the profit this brings him:

> Ful swetely herde he confessioun,
> And plesaunt was his absolucioun:
> He was an esy man to yeve penaunce,
> *Ther as he wiste to have a good pitaunce*. (221–4)

Another way of making his verse more interesting was for the medieval poet to express a simple idea in an elaborate and roundabout manner. On page 53 we saw how Chaucer tells us that his Doctor was a moderate and careful eater. In the case of the Franklin the poet uses twenty-one lines to say that the Franklin was very fond of food. The Miller's big, brawny, uncouth appearance is described in fifteen lines with the help of several telling comparisons. But perhaps the best example of this particular ' colour of rhetoric ' is in the first eighteen lines of the Prologue, all one sentence, and probably the most familiar portion of the whole work. Chaucer says in effect little more than that in mid-April people like to go on pilgrimages, particularly to Canterbury, yet the description becomes beautiful by being thus extended and decorated.

From these examples, then, we see something of Chaucer's careful choice and use of words, their employment in simple, conversational manner at one end of the scale, and in various figures of speech and elaborately ' rhetorical ' passages at the other end. If you read the Prologue carefully you will find many more examples and become more and more impressed by the skill with which Chaucer devoted himself to the poet's art.

For further reading: A valuable critical study is *Geoffrey Chaucer* by N. Coghill. (Writers and their Work: No. 79). Published for the British Council and the National Book League. London, 1956. See also Part II, Chapters 1 and 2, of *Chaucer the Maker* by J. Speirs, London, 1951; and the other books listed on page 73.

Questions:
1.   The first eighteen lines of the Prologue are a lengthy elaboration of a very simple idea. Find other examples of such elaboration and show what kind of detail Chaucer adds.
2.   Which details of style do you think contribute most to the effectiveness of the Prologue as a poem?

3. *Chaucer's Art of Portraiture*
A painter wishing to paint a person's portrait can set about his task in various ways. He can concentrate on the face or show the whole figure; he can paint details of dress or submerge the clothes in shadows; he can add a background showing the person in a distinctive setting, or merely paint a wall or a backcloth or no background at all.

Chaucer's portraits of the Canterbury pilgrims are varied in much the same way, and as the painter uses colours so Chaucer uses the ' colours of rhetoric ' to achieve variety and interest. No two portraits are alike, and there is not one that is complete in the sense that it tells us absolutely everything there is to be known about the person. In every case Chaucer selects

points of detail which appear to him significant about
the person's appearance or character or background.
We might call them ' salient ' details, which means
that they are prominent enough to give us some
impression of the person and distinguish him or her
from others. The fact that the Cook enjoyed drinking
ale (382) he shared with other pilgrims, but the fact

that on his shyne a mormal hadde he (386)

makes him unique among the pilgrims; and it is probably by this fact that we most easily remember him.

Again, as with the use of figures of ' rhetoric ',
there were certain conventions current among medieval
writers about the way to describe a person, some of
them learnt from classical writers like Cicero, others
based on medieval medicine, and so on. Some of the
hints which Chaucer learnt in his way he uses very
readily in the Prologue. For example, medieval
medicine tended to classify people rather in the same
way in which we use terms of modern psychology to
describe them, like ' neurotic ' which means rather
unstable and nervy, or ' unbalanced '. If we use such
a term to-day we imply quite a number of characteristics which go with it, so that to call a person ' neurotic ' is almost a portrait in miniature. Medieval
medicine worked along rather similar lines. It taught
that a person's constitution or temperament depended
on the way in which the bodily elements (they were
called *humours*, as in line 421)

of hoot, or coold, or moyste, or drye (420)

were proportioned. The proportion decided whether
a person was balanced or in some way ' unbalanced ',

E

perhaps jolly and easy-going like the *sangwyn* Franklin
(333), or short-tempered and disagreeable like the
colerik Reeve (587). A mention of such a ' medical '
word was quite enough to indicate a person's character
to a medieval audience, and Chaucer several times
uses this method thereby allowing himself more space
to fill in details of the particular pilgrim's background.
In the Franklin's case this takes the form of a description of the man's many favourite dishes, in the Reeve's
of the latter's methods of administering his master's
property to his own advantage.

Another medieval convention was to describe a
person's appearance systematically downwards from
head to toes, which we have in a nutshell in two lines
of the Merchant's portrait:

> Upon his heed a Flaundryssh bever hat,
> His bootes clasped faire and fetisly.   (272–3)

Yet another began with a person's character, leaving
looks and clothes till later, much as Chaucer himself
says before he begins on the first portrait:

> Me thynketh it acordaunt to resoun
> To telle yow al the condicioun
> Of ech of hem, so as it semed me,
> And whiche they weren, and of what degree,
> And eek in what array that they were inne.
>
> (37–41)

The Knight's portrait, which follows, adheres very
closely to this pattern. It tells us first that he was a
knight (his *condicioun*), then what sort of man he was in
terms of character (*whiche they weren*), then his professional and social background which consists largely

of lists of campaigns (*of what degree*), and finally describes his horse and clothes (*array*).

Although Chaucer was ready enough to learn from his wide reading, he was no slavish follower of literary conventions; hence the different methods of description which he employs in the Prologue and the delightful variety of pilgrims which results.

Some portraits, like the Merchant's, depend on simple enumeration of details of appearance, clothes, and professional skill, although an unexpected touch may be added by the poet, like the fact that the Merchant is in debt which personal observation could not have revealed. Other portraits use the same ingredients but mix them up in order to create the impression of a more composite character, like the Wife of Bath's, in which striking personal features are noted at intervals amid such things as her occupation, her snobbery, her past history, and her present interests.

The interdependence of the various portraits is shown by the numerous contrasts Chaucer draws between one pilgrim and another; so much so that contrast becomes in fact one of Chaucer's principal methods of portraiture and characterisation. The contrast may be in very general terms, as between the conscientious Parson and the unscrupulous Pardoner; or between the two prominent women among the pilgrims, the Prioress and the Wife of Bath. Sometimes a contrast is suggested by a specific detail, as between the Friar's

> For ther he was nat lyk a cloysterer
> With a thredbare cope, as is a povre scoler,
> But he was lyk a maister or a pope.
> Of double worstede was his semycope, (259–62)

and the Clerk's

> Ful thredbare was his overeste courtepy;
> For he hadde geten hym yet no benefice,
> Ne was so worldly for to have office.
> For hym was levere have at his beddes heed
> Twenty bookes, clad in blak or reed. . .
> Than robes riche.   (290–6)

This contrasting method also works in another way. One of Chaucer's favourite ways of characterising a pilgrim is to apply to him in fun some memorable phrase or line already used in all seriousness of someone else. Hence we get such memorable contrasts as

> He was a verray, parfit gentil knyght,
>   (Knight, 72)
>
> He was a verray, parfit praktisour   (Doctor, 422)
>
> Curteis he was, lowely, and servysable,
>   (Squire, 99)
>
> Curteis he was and lowely of servyse. (Friar, 250)

This method is sometimes elaborated by Chaucer's introducing some pointed variation so that the echo of an earlier line becomes even subtler. When we are told that the Parson

> ne maked him a spiced conscience   (526)

our momentary surprise vanishes when we compare Chaucer's intention here with the unmistakable meaning in the Shipman's portrait in a line which the above is meant to recall:

> Of nyce conscience took he no keep.   (398)

Such echoes often depend upon the use of what we have called 'keywords' in certain portraits. The Knight, as we have seen, is the model of true *worthynesse*, and one way of stressing this is Chaucer's repetition of *worthy* and *worthynesse* five times in the course of the Knight's portrait. We therefore associate the word quite properly with the Knight and are rightly suspicious of it when it is applied to the Friar (243), twice to the Merchant (279, 283), and even to the Wife of Bath, ' a worthy womman al hir lyve ' (459), whose *worthynesse* is surely tempered by some very conspicuous shortcomings. Or are we in her case to be reminded of the ' worthy wommen ' whose company Friar Hubert so much enjoyed (217)?

When we read the Prologue in this way Chaucer's achievement must strike us as all the greater, for instead of a series of isolated and independent character sketches we are constantly reminded that this crowd of jostling pilgrims invite comparison with one another and help to set off one another's strong and weak points. Indeed, we judge them in relation to one another: the Pardoner and the Summoner might not have appeared quite so depraved if we had had only the Monk and Friar to compare them with, but the Parson's saintly example shows up each despicable weakness. That such was Chaucer's intention the repeated contrasts between the pilgrims, both in general terms and in specific details, make quite clear. One further result of this interdependence of the various portraits is to add some dramatic interest to the Prologue's portrait parade itself, for the essence of drama is the interaction of different characters. Again we are reminded that the Prologue is more than a mere

list of *dramatis personae* for *The Canterbury Tales*; that
it is in fact the opening scene of the comedy.

The lifelikeness of most of the Canterbury pilgrims
has given rise to several scholarly attempts at identifying them among Chaucer's known contemporaries at
which I have already hinted. Does it not seem probable
that certain pilgrims were in fact modelled upon actual
fourteenth-century Englishmen, although Chaucer
would never hesitate to add touches of his own where
this seemed to him artistically desirable? The Host
of the Tabard Inn, later in *The Canterbury Tales* called
Herry Bailly most probably pictures an actual fourteenth-
century Southwark innkeeper called Henry Bailly; and
here and there are scattered throughout the portraits
hints of possible actual persons. One can think of
several personal features so distinctive that one feels
that Chaucer's own observation noticed them some-
where in real life; but more often it is the occurrence of
a name that adds lifelikeness to a portrait: the Shipman
hails from Dartmouth and is master of the barge
' Maudelayne '; the Reeve comes from Bawdswell in
Norfolk; the Merchant's trading interests were largely
concentrated in Middelburg in Holland and Orwell
near Harwich; the Knight had taken part in campaigns
some of which were topical in 1386 in connection
with a famous lawsuit in which a knightly family
known to Chaucer was involved. Such details of
names of persons or places may well derive from
Chaucer's own knowledge, and with them some of the
particulars of the persons described, and it is certainly
no discredit to Chaucer's art if he did derive some of
his inspiration from living people. With a poet so
very interested in human beings it could hardly be

otherwise. To have so vividly recreated some of his contemporaries among the immortal Canterbury assembly, if this is what Chaucer did in certain cases, is no less an achievement than to have invented the rest.

For further reading: *Some New Light on Chaucer*, by J. M. Manly, New York, 1951, presents some of the most interesting attempts at identifying the pilgrims among Chaucer's contemporaries.

Questions:
1. Discuss Chaucer's use of contemporary science as a means of portraiture in the Prologue.
2. Compare the methods of portraiture used by Chaucer in the case of the following pairs: (*a*) Yeoman and Merchant; (*b*) Clerk and Manciple; (*c*) Squire and Miller.

4. *Chaucer's Humour*
Chaucer's humour is not of the side-splitting kind. He does not tell jokes and expect us to laugh at them. His is a subtle variety which inspires and pervades the whole poem and constantly provides us with new enjoyment.

Primarily Chaucer's humour in the Prologue derives from the fact that he is himself one of the pilgrims, one of the original twenty-nine. He is both actor and spectator and both he and we (his audience) enjoy the antics which this clever arrangement enables him to perform.

We saw on pages 48-9, in mentioning the tags which now and then complete the lines of verse, that

Chaucer often uses these opportunities to remind us of his presence among the pilgrims. But these re- minders were too important to be left merely to occasional tags. Hence we find that in practically every portrait the poet-pilgrim recalls his presence as our guide and interpreter. Sometimes he speaks in his own person, like a reporter (as in 42, 117, 183, 330, 454, 524, 691, and so on); but at other times he sud- denly discards his role as fellow-pilgrim and becomes the omniscient author, that is the real-life creator of all these puppets about whom he of course knows all there is to know. We, the readers, share this delightful game of make-believe in which at one moment we join him as pilgrim while at the next we go into a little private huddle with Chaucer the poet to discover something about one of the characters which none of the other pilgrims could possibly know, but which adds something important to our impression of the person concerned. An obvious example is one already mentioned on page 59, namely the knowledge we share with the poet that the Merchant is in debt:

Ther wiste no wight that he was in dette,   (280)

or how the Prioress intoned the office of divine service which she would not do outside her convent:

Ful weel she soong the service dyvyne,
Entuned in hir nose ful semely.   (122–3)

That Chaucer enjoyed this game is clear also from the witty manner in which he introduces himself to us and asks us to forgive any shortcomings he may have as a reporter:

> But first I pray yow, of youre curteisye,
> That ye n'arette it nat my vileynye,
> Thogh that I pleynly speke in this mateere,
> To telle yow hir wordes and hir cheere,'
> Ne thogh I speke hir wordes proprely.   (725-9)

He honours his audience by relying upon its *curteisye*
as much as he so delightfully humbles himself a few
lines further on.

> My wit is short, ye may wel understonde.   (746)

Of all this motley company it is the poet who has to
apologise for his literary shortcomings! This comic
pose of modesty and literary incompetence is kept up
by the poet throughout *The Canterbury Tales* and
remains a source of frequent delight. Another and
deeper reason for it is that Chaucer was able in this way
thinly to disguise a good deal of the originality and
unconventionality which went into the making of the
Prologue. He deliberately departs from the artificial,
lifeless forms of traditional portraiture (such as he had
himself used in some of his earlier work) in favour of
strikingly realistic or lifelike portrayals; he deliberately ignores some of the subtleties of contemporary
social classification (743-5) no doubt for the sake of
greater dramatic effect; and he here and there voices
opinions which were either too critical or too uncon-
ventional for his courtly audience to be uttered without
the saving excuse that

> my wit is short, ye may wel understonde.

That Chaucer promises to be a genial companion is
plain from the start of the Prologue:

> I was of hir felaweshipe anon,   (32)

and again and again as he presents his fellow-pilgrims to us does his geniality and good humour appear, as we saw when considering the portraits in detail.

The passing of witty comments upon the pilgrims (like ' this Manciple sette hir aller cappe ', 586), or the frequent occasions when he lavishes praise upon some knave while his tongue is practically boring a hole through his cheek, these are the moments when Chaucer's brand of humour comes fully into its own. Sometimes a double meaning which his medieval audience would at once grasp might elude us, as when in the Clerk's portrait the poet plays on the word *philosophre* in its double sense of true ' philosopher ' and ' alchemist ' (someone who seeks to turn ordinary metal into gold):

> But al be that he was a philosophre,
> Yet hadde he but litel gold in cofre.   (297–8)

But there is so much that we to-day can still enjoy that we need not grieve over subtleties which the passage of six hundred years has blunted. Not least among the manifestations of Chaucer's humour, and one which we can all easily enough discern, is the quality of exaggeration which attaches to quite a few of the pilgrims. The merry Friar with his twinkling eyes is ' the beste beggere in his hous ' (252) and ' a noble post ' to his Order; the Franklin has not his equal:

> Was nowher swich a worthy vavasour,   (360)

nor has the Doctor:

> In al this world ne was there noon hym lik;
> (412)

and as for the Shipman:

> Ther nas noon swich from Hulle to Cartage
>
> (404)

And with a stroke so typical of his art, Chaucer crowns all these lines by adding another where he really earnestly means every word he says:

> A bettre preest I trowe that nowher noon ys.
>
> (524)

In these sudden shifts of mood—from the ridiculous to the sublime and back to the ridiculous; from a moment of moving sincerity to one of mockery; from earnest criticism of social abuses and human depravity to poking fun at some harmless folly or ridiculous piece of clothing,—herein lies the true humour of Chaucer which makes the Prologue to *The Canterbury Tales* one of the most charming and justly enduring works of English literature.

For further reading see the general list of books on p. 72.

Questions:

1. Write an essay on ' Chaucer often writes with his tongue very much in his cheek.'

2. Consider Chaucer's use of exaggeration in his description of some of the pilgrims. Have you found any evidence of the opposite device, understatement?

V. Conclusion

Chaucer's poetry is sometimes referred to as 'quaint' or 'naïve'. By now we have discussed the Prologue sufficiently to realise by its art and its lasting appeal that Chaucer was a great poet. Hence such words as 'quaint' or 'naïve' cannot in all honesty be applied to him, unless we mean simply that his language, being six hundred years younger than ours to-day, looks odd to us. This is true, but a little imagination and some effort and practice will help us to regard his language as no less natural and no less mature than Shakespeare's or that of any other English poet or playwright. Admittedly, Chaucer was writing his poems at a time when English had only recently emerged as the language of courtly literature from the long supremacy of Norman French, but he does not give one the impression that his language was in any way so fresh and delicate and fragile that it had to be handled with special care.

If our study of Chaucer's portraits and his art in the Prologue has shown anything at all, it is surely the very opposite, namely real confidence in the choice and use of words, and ability to range with ease from one extreme of language usage to another, that is from colloquial words of everyday usage to learned, technical words relating to law or medicine, and to moments of sheer poetry:

And smale foweles maken melodye,

That slepen al the nyght with open ye,   (9–10)

And have a mantel roialliche ybore,   (378)

Bretful of pardoun, comen from Rome al hoot.

(687)

As a poet Chaucer had no other tools besides words. It took a great poet to use them so well that he can delight and entertain us and make us think seriously with the help of the English of six hundred years ago.

Chaucer's work, like any other artist's, has its short-comings. He moves on too quickly sometimes to remember some flaw left uncorrected or some gap left unfilled, like the missing portraits of the Nun and the Nun's Priest. And *The Canterbury Tales* is not the only one of Chaucer's major poems left unfinished.

The characteristic Chaucerian tag is not an un-mixed blessing either, for however much we may value it in some contexts, as when Chaucer adds his little personal reminders, we may feel at other times that the poet was taking the easy way out. Instead of adding to the meaning of a context he simply slips in some harmless, empty phrase which completes the line and allows him to get on with the business of the next one. Fortunately, the business of the next line is more often than not so interesting or entertaining that the empty tag is forgotten almost as soon as read.

Hand in hand with this go the favourite words and phrases with their tendency to slip in unobserved, like *faire* or *fetys* or *wel koude he*, which are in danger of growing stale after we have met them a few times.

But these are not major defects and although to be aware of them may make us more critical readers of Chaucer's verse, it will not belittle the greatness of Chaucer's poetic achievement.

This achievement must be measured primarily in terms of Chaucer's use of language as we have seen. But other things are also relevant. We cannot know much about fourteenth-century England without

much patient and scholarly study of the social and
political scene, the institutions, customs, and beliefs
of the time. But here, in the Prologue to *The Canterbury Tales* Chaucer has recreated a moment of the fourteenth century set in a corner of England which still
treasures its Pilgrims' Way and its great cathedral at
Canterbury. It is not an exhaustive picture of the age,
but it is a unique glimpse into medieval English
society and into the hearts and minds of men and
women as they then were. The pilgrims are alive and
are placed before us in a dramatic way; we know the
colours of their clothes and watch their table manners;
we share their ambitions as much as their holiday
mood. This variety, this dramatic vividness, and the
lasting charm of this fourteenth-century *compaignye of
sondry folk* are all part of Chaucer's achievement.

Finally there is the delightful figure of Chaucer
himself, both behind the poem and part of it. At one
moment he moves among his pilgrims as one of them,
the next he surveys them from outside or from above
as mere puppets dancing to his strings. With superb
skill the poet parades before our eyes human weaknesses with which we sympathise, foibles at which we
laugh, sins which we condemn, virtues which we
applaud. And the important thing of course is that
these weaknesses and foibles and sins and virtues are
still the same to-day: were we to gather a coach-load
of trippers for a day's outing to the seaside in twentieth-
century England, we should not find any pardoners
or yeomen among them, but might there not be a
quiet, scholarly university don, and a gentle vicar
from a nearby parish, and a self-important business
man and some confidence trickster or slick salesman?

And haven't we all met some big, jolly woman with an enormous picture hat, rather like the Wife of Bath? It is sometimes said that all great poetry has some universal quality about it, some appeal which does not age. In the case of the Prologue it is surely the fact that so many of the things which Chaucer observes and says about his pilgrims are still true to-day. And we accept both his praise and his blame all the more readily because we realise that the charm and tolerance and abundance of good humour are the marks of a lovable though by no means uncritical personality.

VI. FURTHER QUESTIONS

1. What is meant by calling the Prologue ' dramatic? ' What means does Chaucer employ to make the poem ' dramatic '?

2. Discuss the impression which Chaucer creates of himself in the Prologue.

3. Some of the portraits in the Prologue rely as much on details which could not have been observed as on direct observation. Discuss Chaucer's purpose in doing this with reference to some of the pilgrims concerned.

4. Consider in some detail the more important devices Chaucer uses to make the Canterbury pilgrimage come alive in the Prologue.

5. Consider the comment that ' the best portraits in Chaucer's Prologue are those of the rogues.'

6. ' There are very few " purple passages " in the poetry of the Prologue.' Do you think this is true, and if so, what reasons can you give for it?

VII. FURTHER SUGGESTED READING

1. *Chaucer in general.*

N. Coghill, *The Poet Chaucer*. Home University Library. Oxford University Press, 1955. (A thoroughly recommendable book.)

D. S. Brewer, *Chaucer*. (Men and Books Series.) London, 1953. (A good, reliable general survey of Chaucer's work.)

G. K. Chesterton, *Chaucer*. London, 1932. (A very stimulating critical study of Chaucer, suitable for more advanced students.)

R. D. French, *A Chaucer Handbook*. 2nd edition, New York and London, 1947. (A useful reference book, with summaries of Chaucer's poems.)

E. Wagenknecht, *Editor, Chaucer. Modern Escays in Criticism*. (A Galaxy Book.) Oxford University Press, New York, 1959. (A handy collection of twenty-six 'classic' essays on Chaucer, stimulating far more enterprising students.)

2. *The Prologue.*

M. Bowden, *A Commentary on the General Prologue to the Canterbury Tales*. New York, 1949. (A detailed study of the Prologue, bringing together much valuable recent scholarship, suitable for more advanced study of the work.)

R. M. Lumiansky, *Of Sondry Folk. The Dramatic Principle in the Canterbury Tales*. University of Texas Press, 1955. (An interesting and often stimulating study of the twenty-three tales and their tellers, with constant reference to the portraits in the Prologue. Suitable for more advanced students.)